ARE WE HAVING FUN YET?

for better or verse
Alaskan poetry by Ted H. Leonard

cover by Chad Carpenter
illustrations by Chad Carpenter (creator of TUNDRA)
and Jamie Smith (creator of FREEZE FRAME)

ALASKA WORD WORKS PUBLISHING COMPANY
Salcha, Alaska

PUBLISHED BY ALASKA WORD WORKS PUBLISHING COMPANY
P.O. Box 51
Salcha, Alaska 99714

First printing July 1997 USA

Library of Congress Catalog Card Number 97-92910
ISBN 0-9641553-4-6

Dedicated with love to Plum
(short for sugar plum, the wife)...
known to the world as Dottie Leonard...
and to me as the light of my life.

Many thanks to Chad Carpenter and Jamie Smith, a pair of outstanding Alaskan cartoonists.

And thanks to Mitzi Thiel for her poems of pioneer Alaska on pages 60 and 61.

ARE WE HAVING FUN YET?
subtitled Fear of flying

She climbed into the tiny plane,
helped up by the pilot's hand.
She feared her prayers had been in vain,
fright's clutch was an icy band.
Her belly tight with unspoken fright,
she gulped back the taste of bile.
The pilot saw her striken face,
she gave him a sickly smile.
He throttled out, the engines roared,
with a lurch they began to move.
They gathered speed across the pond,
tight clenched fingers were growing sore.
The towering spruce loomed straight ahead,
she muttered a silent prayer,
convinced that she would soon be dead,
that her crashing end was near.
With a stomach gripping, jarring lurch,
the plane broke free at last.
She wished she'd spent more time in church,
and had a purer past.
Into the air at sixty degrees,
it seemed impossibly steep,
the plane leapt up and cleared the trees.
Her knuckles were snowy white.
The plane laid up on its side,
and went into a tight turn.
She lifted her hands up to the roof,
her stomach began to churn.
Her sheer will power held up the plane,
or so it seemed to her.
The pilot then glanced back and laughed,
"You needn't hold it up."
"I promise you, a solemn vow,
it will stay aloft by itself."
And so she became a seasoned flier,
who climbs in without fear.
And nonchalantly takes the flight in stride,
beaming with good cheer.
But if you watch her close, you'll see,
her lips moving in prayer.

MIDLIFE

Many years once lay ahead,
an endless treasure it seemed.
Fifty now, I'm filled with dread.
What became of all I dreamed?

Where did that endless treasure go?
Did I mush those huskies, across the snow?
dig for gold with my bare hands?
explore exotic tropic sands?

Did I write a book, craft a verse?
No!

They slip by so fast, those precious years,
forever gone, too late for tears.
But it's not *too* late, a few remain.
I'll see tropic seas and France and Spain.

I'll waste no more, I'll write my book,
and song and verse, and dig for gold.
And when, at last, my tale is told,
no regrets - I will have lived my dreams.

FEATHERED DEMONS?

Each fisherman has some very odd hooks,
that seem like escapees from Dr. Seuss books.
Birthday gifts from his children (the joy of his life),
or sweet tokens from his affectionate wife,
chosen with love... but without angler's skill,
some are so dreadful they give him a chill.

There's a hideous monster of sickly green hue,
with bulging pop-eyes of electric blue,
a red floating squid, though we're far from the sea
(the lake trout all hid, and chuckled with glee),
bristling oddities of peach... crimson... chartreuse,
a tiny sink with propellors ...
something crafted from moose.

Do you suppose these things star in odd fishy dreams,
nightmares that end in shrill fishy screams?

illustration by Chad Carpenter

FRUITLESS TOIL

I bought two little apple trees,
not much higher than my knees.
I carried them home with pride
to plant them by my cabin side.

There were visions in my mind's eye
of apple sauce and apple pie.
I tended them all summer long,
but mother nature did me wrong.

Each grew to be a healthy tree.
But one day I glanced out to see
a passing moose without a care
take one big bite and strip them bare.

Naught remained but two bare stems
of my ravished little gems.
Next time I vowed I'd have the sense,
to build myself a big high fence

FISHING THE ARCTIC NIGHT

Soft, golden, glows the Arctic night.
Golden glows the crystal creek,
reflecting clouds of peach and rose
in the soft, blue, midnight sky.

My fly line casts a graceful arc.
Some beavers swim upstream.
Bald eagle sits, white head aglow.
It all seems like a dream.

Momma moose comes strolling out to drink,
with two tiny newborn calves.
And along the bank a playful mink
splashes in and out.

All God's creatures are out tonight,
sporting about with glee,
putting on an awesome show,
just for me to see.

So, as solstice gives us glowing nights,
give up an evening's sleep.
Get out and see God's midnight sights,
a treasure you can keep.

CHATNIKA DAYS

I was wandering out Chat-nika way,
when I heard a noise like a fast moving sleigh,
whistling across the crusted snow,
moving along faster than I could go.

I spun around and got a bit of a fright,
at the remarkable, unexpected sight
of a homey old outhouse that had learned to ski,
a brown blur of speed, bearin' down on me.

The door hung wide open and I plainly could see
inside sat a sourdough grinnin' at me.
I jumped in the snow bank and covered my head
cowering down in terrible dread.

This, I knew, was not my way to die —
run down by an outhouse for not bein' spry.
So I struggled and rolled, fought my way free,
and hid myself out behind a spruce tree.

Not from cowardice, as Plum will claim,
but because I couldn't bear the shame...
called to my maker, ahead of my time,
cut down by an outhouse, while still in my prime.

illustration by Chad Carpenter

KACHEMAK BAY - Tranquillity

Deep blue mountains loom on high,
against the sky blue dome,
with mighty glaciers on their flanks,
like bluish smoky haze.
Wisps of cloud are scattered round,
and there - off north toward home,
a fire shot plume, volcanic smoke,
reflects red morning rays.

Deep blue waters of the bay,
reflect a reddish path.
It leads on out, into the gulf,
like sailing in a dream,
of blue on blue, cupped in blue,
with just a touch of red,
and Dawn's first touch upon the waves,
causing them to gleam.

Deep breaths bring in the fresh salt air,
with welcome seaweed tang,
a scent of fish, and from the land,
the bracing scent of spruce.
And on the air, the seagull's cry,
the bobbing bell buoy's clang,
the whispering rush of water split,
moving from our way.

Deep felt, the sting of driving spray,
the cold of morning breeze,
brings the senses all alert,
the soul is at it's ease.
Oh take me back to Kachemak,
to Homer and the spit.
It is a place where I'm at peace,
a place where I can fit.

KACHEMAK BAY - Razor Clamming

I got out here at five o'clock,
I thought we would be first.
Low tide was not 'til six A.M.,
but, gosh, just look at them.

A bustling band, swarms on the sand,
already hard at work,
digging for the razor clam,
the tide is minus three.

I smiled at her, she smiled at me,
and then I took her hand.
We scampered cross black sucking mud,
and on, to firmer sand.

And all around, the dimpled sand,
betrayed the clam at home.
We dug right in, to chase them down,
my hand came up all brown.

The clinging mud, brought out a frown,
and she said, "eew yuck.";
but to catch a clam, you must get down,
and wallow in the muck.

I persuaded her, she got right in,
to the spirit of the thing -
laughed and squealed and wallowed 'round,
she was a sight to see.

But when we got back to the shore,
she looked into a mirror,
and then my name was really mud.
Boy, was she ever sore!

KACHEMAK BAY - The fishing trip

At minus five, the tide is out,
a drop of thirty feet.
The floating docks lie far below,
the ramps seem awful steep.
I swallow hard, looking down,
I promised myself this treat.
Down the ramp I force myself,
onto the boat I leap.
Beyond the spit are rolling waves,
I force myself aboard.
The captain heard me mumbling,
a prayer to the Lord,
"I came out for the halibut,
not to go to my reward."
"The waves are not too bad," he said.
His smile conveyed good cheer.
Looking at the three foot swell,
I consoled me with a beer.
We bounced on out through rising seas;
for this I paid good cash?!

An hour or more away from shore,
the anchor made a splash.
I took the rod, the bait went down,
into the raging sea.
In the rolling boat and five foot waves,
up and down went the bait,
In rising wind and rising sea,
breakfast deserted me.
And yet, and still, I felt a thrill,
a tug of a heavy weight.
I fought it in, with tired arms,
my rod was sharply bent.
A monstrous halibut came to gaff,
two hundred pounds he went.
Then we turned, and ran for shore,
through angry towering seas,
I puked and puked, three hours or more,
and landed with wobbly knees.
Please take me back to Kachemak,
I want to go back for more.

illustration by Jamie Smith

ZIP?

Of taste the Post Office has a lack,
they say that I live in... AK?
Washington, once a very proud name,
now has WA as its claim to fame.
And Texas, big and sprawling land,
becomes wimpy TX at the Postmaster's hand.
Wyoming, land of scenic wonders,
turns to WY?
It's enough to make you cry.

AK? that's not where I live.
Alaska, I insist, is the name you give.
Efficiency and progress is mighty fine...
but, at AK, I draw the line.

WEATHER OR NOT

It's doing it's usual the weathermen say.
Clouding up Fridays, like it's been doing since May.
Saturday will be rainy and stormy and gray.
And Sunday will bring downpour;
it makes me so sore.
Monday? Partly clearing, that's their advice.
Tuesday through Thursday? They'll be very nice.
The cycle repeats, time after time.
Nice weekdays, crummy weekends, it should be a crime.
One thing for sure, you'll oft hear me say,
"Count on it. I'm going fishing today...
weather or not it's stormy and gray.

LEAVE ME ALONE
There has always been a frontier.

I roam among the frozen wastes,
lands not quite to others' tastes.
A harsh, deserted, alien land
that I have come to love.
Free, from its mountains to the sand.

There has always been a frontier.
A place for those who have no fear
of the wilderness without,
nor, yet, of the wilder wilderness
that lurks within each one.
A place for those with courage to be free.

There has always been a frontier.
For those who dislike close social bounds,
excessive rules and long nosed fools,
swarming crowds and blare of sounds.
Now the simpering, whimpering, cowardly fools,
are huddled in desolate urban wastes,
loving detailed, voluminous, pervasive rules
to govern every act

You want to paint your house a sunny yellow?
better ask your neighboring fellow
to check the block association rules
and give you permission from the fools.
And what? You want to fly the flag?
Careful, it may make them gag.

They don't want our barren waste,
but still they make unseemly haste
to destroy our freedom to wander here.
What is it, do you guess, they fear?
There has always been a frontier.
A place for those who love to be free.
Alaska was this country's last,
a relic of the country's past.

Now what is left? ... After your sin.
With bureaucrats, you have caged us in.
Careful, we may yet have the heart,
to take your society all apart.

and make us room to be free

NOW! WE'RE HAVING FUN
(an Alaskan saying, in times of adversity)

Dreary, dark, dismal, dripping,
from sullen brooding skies;
daunting, drenching, steady rain,
upon the foliage sighs.
From each leaf, each tree and bush,
damp, dank drizzles drain.
Grim, grey, gulches gushing rain,
rain puddles on the flat,
mushy, moldy, squishy moss,
and on the creek, a steady splat.
I travel on, a plodding pace,
I really feel like heck.
I brush the water from my face,
it's dripping down my neck.
Dripping, draining, from my hat,
it's dampening my shirt.
Pants seat wet, where I sat,
when I fell on slippery dirt;
pants legs, wet from dripping brush,
are stuffed in rain filled boots.

We came out on this camping trip,
in the land of midnight sun.
I trudge on through the steady drip,
Now! we're having fun

illustration by Jamie Smith

JUST MY LUCK

I know I must be out of gas,"
the boater told the pretty lass,
"We've come so far it must be gone.
I'll fill her up again."

He put the drum up on the chair,
lined up the siphon hose with care.
With resignation he eyed that hose
and said, "Bless me dear...here goes."

He gave the hose a mighty suck,
but the poor devil was out of luck.
A mighty gush the boater drank,
but none found its way inside the tank.

That was written from painful personal experience.
Does it ring a bell for anyone else?...Ah-ha, I thought so.

ARCTIC HUNTRESS' DAY

Among cottonwood's great golden puffs,
mixed with deep green spruce;
are scattered, brilliant, crimson strokes,
leaves of the currant bush.
Warm golden rays, fall on the rock,
frost vanishes as steam.

Frost sharpened blow, the scents of fall;
perfuming the faintest breeze.
She crouches there, beside me now,
With bated breath we watch.
Grey ghosts appear, in the morning mist,
from nowhere, as in a dream.

With widened eyes, and nostrils flared,
blood surging, hot in her veins;
she lifts her rifle, holds it tight.
It speaks, a crashing boom.
Mighty horns jerk up, and freeze;
then fall, and disappear.

She leaps, and runs, to the brush,
she parts it, and she sees.
She turns and calls, in a high sweet voice,
"A big one, and he's dead!"
I see her strut, coming back,
across the broken ground.

At camp that night, the meat was hung.
The stars stood crisp and bright.
Her hand crept snuggling, into mine,
in the still of night.
Ruddy campfire flickered, as we sat,
well content with the day, and our life.

LYIN' LEFTY'S MOOSE

Like fishermen, the hunters, too,
are known for tales that aren't quite true.
Of them all, Lyin' Lefty's are worst.
He tells each one unrehearsed;
quite impromptu, if you will,
like the day he boasted a fresh kill.

"I killed it with one shot," he said.
"A single shot left it lying dead."
His partner spluttered in amaze,
giving him an unbelieving gaze,
and said, "Don't you find it quite uncouth,
to utter such a bold untruth."

"You emptied out your gun,
and missed with every one --
but the last, which knocked him dead,
with a lucky shot to the head."
Lefty capered about with glee
and chortled, "There, now you see."

"I killed it with a single shot.
whether you believe it, or not."
Put that way, I had to agree,
"One shot is all it ever takes me...
The last, of course," I said with a frown,
"Why keep on shooting, once he's down."

CAUSE AND EFFECT

Did you ever notice, when you think about
maybe taking your fly rod out,
how a gentle breeze begins to blow...
a hint of warning to those who know.

And when you begin to strip some line
the wind will gust, a rising whine.
And when you make a cast, or three,
wild storm warnings go up at sea.

The truth is out, without a doubt,
and the truth is this, I hope to shout:
A persistent angler who takes the pains
can easily stir up hurricanes.

THE CALL OF THE WILD

I roam among the arctic peaks,
along the bubbling icy creeks.
To all who ask I do declare,
"I seek the gold that's buried there."

And yet, if pressed, I would admit,
the lure of gold isn't all of it.
For the greatest treasure, in my esteem
is precious days spent by the stream.

Spruce and birch, lovely trees,
are blowing in the whisp'ring breeze.
Underneath, yellow tundra rose
wafts its perfume to my nose.

Lightning flash and grey skies chill,
cause my every sense to thrill.
And when the grey gives way to blue,
so the sun shines - a golden hue,

Then I bask in its rays so mild,
thankful for my days in the wild.
I see caribou and moose at play,
and fox and mink and wolf so grey.

Oh grizzly bear, you shambling brute,
go away, don't make me shoot.
With grouse and jays the woods are rife,
and squirrels amongst their teeming life.

And at night, by my campfire's light,
orange and flickering, leaping, bright
- I sit there warm, by the fire,
and know I've found my heart's desire.

illustration by Jamie Smith

ARCTIC MADNESS

She sketched on a blank white pad.
Outside the window, the lonely birch
thrust skeletal fingers into off-white skies.
Stark, dreary, black, the dwarf forest loomed,
against silent, repellent, dead white.
Twisted, tortured, permafrost trees,
a mirror of her soul.
Moaning wind sobbing through the spruce
broke the silence of the North.
She sat and stared into the mid-day gloom.

Coming in for lunch, he found her there,
amongst dirty breakfast plates.
Frightened by her unfocussed stare,
he studied her self portraits and saw
flat, dead eyes — unkempt, stringy hair
hanging down 'round an expressionless face.

The chilling pictures, he knew, reflected the state of her soul.
Arctic madness had struck again, cabin fever, as it is known.
There was no way to make her whole, but a trip to a warmer land
He'd take her away, without delay, he rushed to the snow-machine.
He labored hard and got it going, although the cold was cruel.

"Jenny," he called, "let's go to town." He wore a happy smile.
Silence answered...
she lay face down in a spreading pool,
of cooling, reddish brown.

YUKON QUEST

Black velvet, the backdrop of Arctic night,
pierced through by points of twinkling white.
Gauzy, glimmering, ghostly, green,
rippling curtains waver across the scene -
And around the pole star, home of the dead,
wavers a curtain of shimmering red.
Now, from the hush of the Arctic night,
grows a sibilant hiss from beyond sight.
Whistling sled runners?... the ghost team's breath?
racing across the sky, undeterred by death.

Arctic Spring

With a whispering elfin tinkle,
lonely cakes of ice collapse,
lying stranded on the gravel,
touched by the springtime sun.

In the golden rays upon the stone,
frost vanishes into steam.
And blows away on the gentle breeze
to vanish like a dream.

The green tinge of pussy willow's bark
and its fuzzy first bloom of spring
bring a message to our frozen land,
a promise of rebirth.

illustration by Jamie Smith

RITES OF SPRING

(late March)
Fresh snow covers my deck and chair
and blankets my barbeque.
But the sky is fair and there's warmth in the air...
why it's gone above thirty-two!

Despite what you say, it's the heat of the day,
in the golden Arctic sun.
Time for swimming suits and breakup boots.
Time to enjoy some springtime fun.

"Swimming suits?" my wimpy wife hoots,
(I call her sugar plum).
"At thirty-three degrees, with an icy breeze,
I really call that dumb."

"And who but a man... I ask you who?
would burn good meat on a barbeque?"
Comments like that are best ignored,
unhearing silence their deserved reward.

Tanning lotion, I briskly rub on my form.
(Brisk rubbing helps to keep you warm.)
Slyly leaning o'er the grill.. to check the meat,
I subtly soak up the charcoals' heat.

Thought I, I must admit it's rather cold.
I wish I hadn't been so bold.
"I hate to see you shivver so," I lied,
"maybe I'd better take you back inside."

FUNNY BUSINESS
(Ted's note to Chad Carpenter on
a rainy day at the Palmer Fair)

She stood by my booksellers booth,
watching others read a while.
Then she spoke a simple truth -
"It's great to make folks smile."

And though we never scorn the cash,
in our business of being funny,
we also seek those extra rewards -
there's easier ways to make money.

So 'toonist Chad, upon your pad,
keep on sketching humor dandy.
Keep on making folks hearts glad -
But keep the cash box handy!!

A FANTASY OF REVENGE

The band played on... and on... and on...
until I swore my mind was gone.
Twelve hours a day, I sat at the fair,
stoically enduring the trumpet's blare.
My hearing aids rang with the awful din --
so, though I knew it was a mortal sin,
I got the gun out of my van...
and shot and killed the music man.

(I sure was tempted)

A CHRISTMAS PLEA

Cookies, candy, things like that,
all contribute to my fat.
It doesn't seem fair to me,
that that's the way things should be.

Everything that's good to taste
ends up growing 'round my waist.
Furthermore, truth to tell,
I gain weight just from the smell.

Merry Christmas, the greeting sounds.
I just gained ten more pounds.
Santa, please, under the tree,
leave some will power just for me.

illustration by Jamie Smith

WARM WISHES from Alaska

It's cold and clear with crusted snow,
minus sixty and the wind will blow.
The stove burns wood we can't afford
— every day nearly half a cord.

Yet Christmas comes only once a year,
a time for joy and for good cheer.
But I really don't understand why,
we couldn't cheer... down in Hawaii.

AND from Hawaii

It's fifty below, the thermometers say.
There the barometer says it'll stay
— cold and clear for Christmas day
and into New Year's, too.
We've seen minus eighty, in the past.
We'll see it again... that's my forecast.
So the reason is plain as plain can be,
why Santa will find us at Waikiki.
Merry Christmas to all.
Happy New year, too.
From tropic sands
and surf so blue.

'NEATH THE MIDNIGHT SUN

Circling 'round the azure dome,
of the northern sky,
never sleeping midnight sun,
lights our arctic home.
Three months long, the golden day,
for a year of work and fun.

Midnight's golden glow oft finds
us still at work or play.
We sleep less now, not to waste,
summer's one long golden day.
Death of summer soon will bring,
autumn's frosty taste.

Summer's one long golden day,
'neath the midnight sun,
fades away to velvet night
and the mid-day moon.
Crackling, wavering, greenish light,
Aurora is at play.

Fifty below, blowing snow,
winter rules the land.
Crisp and cold, approaching spring,
every day at noon,
with brief, grey hours of dim light,
promises rebirth.

APRIL ICE

Harridan river, making display
of Winter's tattered finery,
long past its time.
Come, join in Spring's renewal.
Cast off your dowdy garments,
sullied now, no longer white.
Be a damned harridan no more.
Instead, dancing debutant,
frolic to the sea.

illustration by Jamie Smith

THE CHEECHAKO AND THE BEAR BELLS

We were sitting 'round the camp,
relaxed and unaware,
soaking in the peace and calm,
from the country air.

Across the creek, we saw a bear
rear up and stand erect.
But we were still without a care,
our bear bells close to hand.

I shook the bells, a ringing sound,
carried clearly to the bear.
Growling, snarling, he turned around.
We began to feel a scare.

He came our way, we were all unnerved.
To him those bells meant dinner was served.
Stealthy like a cat he crept,
gliding through the brush.

We backed away from the camp.
We huddled in a bunch.
Fearfully, we watched the bear,
gobble up our lunch.

You may have heard that bears mean no harm.
That they are cute creatures full of charm.
That they harbor no malice, and it is true,
only when hungry, will they eat you.

TOK SPOKE

Most roads have two ends,
like a piece of string,
a river, a yard stick,
or any old thing.

But the Alaska Highway,
if you know the score,
has... not two... not three...
but four.

One end lies south
at Dawson Creek.
The others?
That depends on to whom you speak.

Fairbanks boasts it is the end,
Delta folks say that
Fairbanks' milepost does offend.

Little Tok's voice joins in the choir,
"Don't apologize
for calling each other a liar.
It's just as plain as plain can be,
the end lies right here with me."

THERE OUGHT TO BE A LAW

"There ought to be a law," he said,
    "to keep you folks in line."
The words drew all eyes in the place
    to the young man's shining face.
A three piece suit and shoes that shine,
    a razor cut for his hair,
the cheechako was clearly fresh arrived
    from the lower forty-eight.

The bearded sourdough met his gaze,
    while leanin' back in his chair
His faded jeans matched his eyes,
    he had wildly straggling hair.
A free and independent spirit,
for enjoying life, the sourdough had a flair.

The old man said, "It's kind of you,
    to share your outsider's lore.
I reckon that it must be great,
now that you've cleaned up your own state;
    and have no more smog in your air
        and no more traffic jams
    or pollution in your streams or sea.
Damned nice of you to come up here,
    just to educate me.

illustration by Jamie Smith

THE ONE THAT GOT AWAY

While driving up the highway,
I saw a mighty moose,
dribbling globs of pond weed
like trapper Ron dribbles snoose.

Now I was up near Cantwell
on my way home from the fair.
And though I hate to say it,
my freezer was mighty bare.

"What's the season? What's the rules?"
I rummaged out the book.
The big bull stood there patient
while I took a hasty look.

And in the book I sadly read,
"The rack must be fifty-five inches
or more across its spread...
or you must leave the moose alive.

Fifty-four? or fifty-six?
So ran my mind's debate.
My mental tape ran round his rack...
Hell! - He'd easy go fifty-eight!

I pulled my rifle to my shoulder.
I had him in my sight.
The knuckle on my finger
turned a snowy white.

But then I held my fire,
recalling how the mind
can grow antlers on the brow
of a thoroughly bare-headed,
luscious looking... cow.

And as I thought, anxiety fraught,
he took a step, then two.
And vanished in the concealing brush.

And then my hunt was through.

JUST A-FISHIN'

Larry wrung his hands and loudly moaned,
"I wish we hadn't slid right in,
I wish we had a tow."

Just then I heard a motor boat,
about to see our woe.

"Now Larry," I said, in urgent tone,
"Just hush up with your wishin'.
Take this rod in your hand...
and pretend we're just a-fishin'."

illustration by Jamie Smith

ARCTIC DAY

Stark black trunks of spruce loom
against all pervasive white.
Delicate, crystalline frost muffles the trees and brush.
Frost silences the world, soft at forty below.
Snowshoes break the silence with muffled crunch.
A form appears, bulky, parka bundled,
traveling, across the lonely land,
breath steaming from the hood.

She stops, parka hood swept back,
her hair ripples...a brilliant flame,
against the colorless land.
Restless emerald eyes scan for signs of life.
Across the whitened plain,
another rippling, brilliant flame springs forth,
twitching sharp nose lifted.
The fox scents the breeze - and freezes in alarm.

The rifle lifts, steadies.
Down the barrel, The emerald eyes gaze.
A puff of smoke. A muffled crack.
Crimson stains the snow.
Forty below steals warmth from the steaming blood.
Elated, she gathers the prize.

The muffled crunch of snowshoes fades toward the tiny cabin.
Silence settles on the land.
White snow, red stained,
tells a silent tale.
Stark black trunks of spruce loom
against all pervasive white.
Delicate, crystalline frost muffles the trees and brush.
Frost silences the world, soft at forty below.

(This poem won the $1,000 grand prize in the Spring 1992 Iliad Press Literary Awards Program.)

ARCTIC CHRISTMAS

Orange flickers of light brighten our ruddy faces.
An orange look of warmth is cast into the room.
As we stoke our barrel stove, frost steams from our clothes.
In my mustache, balls of ice melt and drip.
Frosty fingers sting with returning blood.
Cheeks burn, toes tingle.

The tea kettle's whistle speaks comfortingly
of steaming mugs.
Hot chocolate, gratefully swallowed, what bliss!
Outside, Northern Lights dance, ghostly green,
great crackling banners streaming across the star lit sky.
Stark, black, spruce embrace our cabin home.

A pot of stew bubbles, sending forth its savory scent.
Orange flickering light, from the stove's open door,
lights the room.
Orange light dances and shines, reflected from our tree,
decorated with tinsel, glass bulbs -- and popcorn
we strung with happy laughter.

Twined in each other's arms, we join in silent thanks
for the peace of our Arctic solitude.
Orange flickers warm our hearts, on Christmas Eve.

TROPIC DAWN

Stretching far to either side,
in tropic pre-dawn grey,
foaming surf outlined in white
the curving beach, Ki-hei.

I stepped into the surging warmth,
it broke with hollow boom.
Black against the morning grey,
I saw Ka-hoo-la-we loom.

Against the slowly greying sky,
the horizon was stark and black.
Sparkling night lights on the coast,
the water reflected back.

I turned to face toward Maui now,
warm surf surged round my knees.
Lovely, exotic, tropic palms,
whispered in the breeze -

every fiber of every frond
silhouetted clear and stark.
A wash of pink grew across the sky,
to slowly banish dark.

Ha-le-a-kala wore a rosy crown,
pink puffs of cloud were west.
Amongst a spreading golden glow,
the sun rose from it's rest.

ARCTIC INTERLUDE

It was minus forty when we left,
our home white shrouded in snow.
Long hours of dark had left their mark,
our spirits were drooping low.

We climbed aboard the jumbo jet,
soared into the icy sky.
As we flew on south through the night,
the moon rose full and high.

We came down through the velvet night
We landed near Waikiki.
Soft tropic moon cast golden light
in a path across the sea.

Silhouetted against the moon,
trembling in warm, perfumed breeze,
the palm trees' fronds whispered soft,
of a life of tropic ease.

Though we love our Arctic home,
cold and dark sometimes make us flee
to tropic palms and tropic sands
and breakers of a tropic sea.

illustration by Jamie Smith

TENTING TONIGHT

I saw the ad about the tent.
To me it sounded heaven sent.
Seven by seven, sleeps three, it said.
Never a doubt entered my head.

My wife and I went camping out.
Putting up that tent was quite a bout.
Connect each pole A to each part B,
hook the whole mess to center part C.

The sagging tent was looking bad,
not a bit like the ad.
A billowing, sagging, drooping mess,
but I said, "It'll do, I guess."

This whole time, rain was pouring down.
I really feared that we might drown.
Along one side, we let her sleeping bag lie,
next a week of food, to keep it dry.

Spare clothes and gear were next inside,
we had to keep them fully dried.
Under the flap I peered to see.
I looked and found no room for me.

illustration by Chad Carpenter

SIGNS OF SPRING

Just in case you hadn't heard,
the mosquito is our national bird.
It isn't colorful - or good to eat
nor is its song a musical treat.

If you ignore the creatures' drone,
next thing you know, you're pierced to the bone
You reach for the Off, Muskol or Cutters
but off out of reach the varmint flutters.

Buzzin' and dronin' and drivin' you mad -
you'll find it hard to be very glad
at the sight of *this* harbinger of spring.
You'd rather kill the damned little thing.

Are we having fun yet?

illustration by Chad Carpenter

FEAR IN THE DARK

Sere yellow leaves are drifting down,
amid fat flakes of snow.
Dark, gloomy clouds cast a chill,
in evening's pearly glow.
Rising wind moans a mournful dirge
for the soul of the fool who roams.
With dark shadows, black tree trunks merge,
where goblins make their homes.

Prickling hair bristles on my neck,
a chill runs up my spine.
Dimly seen movements in the dusk —
a howl — a wolf wants to dine.
In the shadows I strain my ears,
do I hear an eager whine?
And does the odor of fallen leaves
cover a grimmer musk?

Points of stars spring into being
against the deepening dusk.
I'm closer now to my cabin door,
I may make it yet.
At my heels, a scrabbling sound,
my heart gives a lurch.
Not close enough, I think in fright,
on survival, I won't bet.

At last I step into the glow
of the cabin's yellow light,
and turn around, to confront
the cause of my fright.
There I see my tame fox,
the one that I keep fed,
standing there on his hind legs,
begging for meat or bread.

Feeling foolish, I laugh aloud
and hasten on inside,
he knows I have some scraps for him,
but I give him steak instead.

STARVATION CREEK
(from the novel Starvation Creek Legacy)

Some Alaskan creeks have a ghastly name,
just think of a few that have some fame:
Coldfoot, No Grub and Deadhorse speak
of hardship, suffering and death;
and on the banks of Starvation Creek?...
Two miners drew their last breath.

Now, Hog River Hanah met Wolfer Joe from Gulkana
on a spree on the Koyukuk.
She told him proud (she got real loud)
that she'd had a little luck.
She'd found some gold and came on to him bold,
when she saw him in Wiseman camp.
And Wolfer Joe, far from feeling low,
thought her an engaging vamp.

(at the time he was loaded with hooch)

She propositioned him plain and he, feeling no pain,
fell right in with her plans,
to share a bed roll as they traveled south
along with their picks and pans.
They went south to Novaksut River,
there to search for gold
where unnamed creeks rush from rocky peaks
through permafrosted wastes and cold.

On one of these creeks they had some luck
(found a placer buried 'neath the muck)
so their fortune seemed mighty fine.
Alas, alack, this was twenty-nine,
the winter spawned in hell.

On Christmas Eve (their diaries tell)
the mercury began to drop
minus eighty-four, the reading was,
when it finally came to a stop.
No moose or caribou, rabbit or bear
moved near the frozen creeks.

It stayed cold far too long, four dreary weeks,
and warmed too late, for they'd met their fate,
starved, then frozen solid.
A wanderer through this land untamed
found them in the spring.
And so Starvation Creek was named
for this ghastly thing.
It lurks in wait until this date,
waiting its next victim.
And now a modern miner comes
do you think it might be him?

THE STORM

A breath of breeze stirred the spruce,
it made the faintest sigh.
An ominous, greenish light,
grew in the western sky.

The rising wind's low pitched wail,
(I was uneasy and alone)
reminded me of the ancient tale,
of the banshee's sobbing moan.

The usual sounds of forest life,
of love and song and strife,
were silent now, nothing heard,
from squirrel, or moose, or bird.

The angry clouds were boiling black,
a purple hue behind.
At lightning's flash, and thunder's crack;
I feared I'd lose my mind.

The rolling booms, the streaks of light,
the shaking of the ground;
I feared I'd lost my ears and sight,
t'was so loud there was no sound.

And then the sun came creeping out,
the sky changed back to blue;
the birds were singing all about,
I saw the rainbow too.

JACK FROST

Jack Frost just nipped my nose,
only moments after he nipped my toes.
He's all about, both here and there,
penetrating my clothes, frosting my hair...

The little pervert!

illustration by Chad Carpenter

MINUS SIXTY

Clumsy hands and stinging face,
it seems I walk on knives.
I still feel, by heavens grace --
Pain's end means only death.

Stiff fingers, feeling warm and nice,
won't bend the way they should.
Put in my mouth, they feel like ice;
to my teeth, they are hard as wood.

Desperate tears sting my eyes
and freeze my lashes tight.
Rubbing helps, but not a lot.
I've begun to lose my sight.

Stumbling, blind, I must keep on.
I fall and rise again,
and stumble toward the Arctic dawn,
stark black, and white, and grey.

And then I fall and can't get up.
The snow seems soft and fine.
I can not bend my arms or legs.
Black ravens line up to dine.

Somehow it doesn't matter now,
my white bed is soft and warm.
It folds me in a soft embrace.
I'll just close my eyes a while.

A WILD RIDE

Old Ben, when he was twenty-one,
an avid sportsman was.
He loved the trout, the grouse, and deer.
He loved to roam the hills.
With venison steak his favorite meal,
he hunted high and low,
for the wily white tail, in the brush;
through rain, or sleet, or snow.
Then came the day, he saw one sneak,
thinking to get away.
His rifle rose, he made it speak;
it echoed from the hills.
He fired once, and thought he'd missed,
though the bullet was in its chest.
The rifle spoke, a ringing boom,
now he thought a head shot best.
Hit on the horn, it knocked it out,
the deer fell to the ground.
It's tongue lolled out, it sure looked dead;
Ben laughed, a happy sound.
He strode right up, astride its neck,
and bent to cut its throat.
The knife's first prick revived the deer.
It jumped up, scared as heck.
Its antler slid up Ben's pant leg,
it's back between his knees.
Away they went, right down the hill,
banging against the trees.
It ran a hundred yards, or so,
Ben said it seemed much more.
It jumped on down a six foot bank,
and made Ben awful sore.
It died right there, upon the trail,
it couldn't go no more.
Ben laid there stunned and looking up,
and feeling rather frail.
Some green clad legs came into view,
green coat and shiny star.
The ranger said, "That's something new,
a-riding one to death."

THE BEST LAID PLANS

We eyeballed out the birch tree,
to see which way it leaned,
gathered up the chain saw,
sharp and tight and cleaned.

Out the window my wife watched.
I could see she was up tight.
But carefully we notched it,
so that birch would fall just right.

We cranked hard on the come-along,
to get the tree to lean.
We hammered in the wedge.
Man! We ain't so green.

Careful planning pays off, they say.
But I can't see any proof.
You see, that darned old birch tree
lit square across the roof.

illustration by Jamie Smith

VOICE OF A PIONEER

These two pages are from Mitzi Thiel. In the early days Mitzi and her husband Victor joined the rush to the Golden Heart of Alaska.

Mitzi writes: I'm 89 years old now and I still recall the Christmas of 1936 as the most exciting Christmas of my life. For, in 1936, a longshoremen's strike cut off all freight to Alaska for three months. It looked like a bleak holiday, as we ran out of supplies, until three boats reached Seward, just in time for Christmas.

Intense excitement swept through Fairbanks when the freight got to town two days before Christmas, including fresh fruit and vegetables. The stores were open 'til midnight Christmas Eve and 'til noon on Christmas day. I wrote the following poem after that wonderful holiday.

JUST IN TIME FOR CHRISTMAS
by Mitzi Thiel (1936)

Now that Christmas Day is over, I take time to pen a line
of all the lovely things we done, at this happy Christmas time.
Things looked very dark and dreary on account of the strike.
According to the papers, its been an awful fight.

But God looked down upon us, and saw our dire need
so three boatloads of provisions, he sent us with some speed
To make Alaskans happy, here in the frozen North
as we sallied about our errands, back and forth.

In October was the last boat, to bring us any freight.
Everybody worried that our freight would come too late.
But the railroad and post office both worked like mad
to give us the merriest Christmas that we have ever had

We had a great big turkey, cooked to a golden brown,
and served him with a cranberry sauce, for he is the boss.
And we had all the fresh stuff, lettuce, bananas and pears.
And with us for that dinner were two friends whom we owed shares.

I baked a fruit cake and also a mince pie
and we all ate until I thought we'd die.
And lots of other welcome things were put beneath our tree.
Things old friends sent on that boat, North to Vic and me.

Down to forty below the weather had been
but Mother Nature now was kind

and brought it back to ten above
Another pleasure we could find.

After all is said and done
it was a wonderful day.
One that I remember
as I go along life's way.

We got twenty-some card and letters in our Christmas mail
from relatives and friends who would never, ever fail
to send us their best wishes, now that we were gone,
and who still love us, as time marches on.

We hope you're well and happy,
Father dear
and we send you our best wishes,
for a very happy New Year.

During World War Two, Mitzi writes, she worked for Pete Despot. Pete
ran the Model Cafe, the biggest restaurant in town. The big influx of
soldiers and airmen meant that swarms of troops were in town to party
every night. So, much of the time, some of the waitresses would party 'til
the wee hours and couldn't make it to work on time (or sometimes at all).
When that happened, Pete would call Mitzi to fill in. She worked some odd
hours.

PETE'S MODEL CAFE
by Mitzi Thiel

I get up in the morning
and start to plan my day.
Then the phone starts ringing
and Uncle Pete will say,
"Can you come in at noon?"
or "Can you come in at four?"
So I drop the things I'm doing
and hurry out the door.
I don't want to be a quitter
and I hope I'm not a cheat.
But today I'll get my freedom...
'cause I'm quitting Uncle Pete!

This next one isn't about Alaska. But it's an interesting look at another
 period

MY FIRST OFFENSE
by Jule Osier (my father-in-law)
circa 1920 (prohibition era)

My name is Jule Osier, they arrested me today.
For driving while drunk, upon the main highway!
Oh! Alfred Ingman is the man that seen me first to hail,
and as an officer, took me to the county jail.

Next morning he took me to the judge, a very nice old man.
'Least everybody says he is, that doesn't know the man.
I stood not knowing what to do, with officers all around.
The judge he looked at me so cross, saying, "take your hat off and sit down."

He got up from a chair with a paper from which he read.
I couldn't talk his language, so did not know what he said.
He looked at me, I looked at him. I said, "I guess you're right."
Although this was my first offense, it wasn't very light.

"One hundred dollar fine," says he. "Or ninety days in jail."
I knew I had no money and it made me feel so pale.
I had to pay with ninety days, I couldn't get the cash.
But being locked up in the jail is not so bad at last.

We have some cards and checker boards and lots of things to read.
But some in here, just visitors, kick on how they feed.
If they, like me, got ninety days, I think they'd call it good.
If they've heard jails had menus, they sure misunderstood.

And when my ninety days are up, and I am still alive,
I'll try to think before I drink, stay sober while I drive.
Now, all you boys that like your drink, you're better not to try,
this little town of Munsing, or you'll get the same as I.

The sheriff, he wants me to tell of where I got my drinks.
I've only been here thirty days, but at every house, I think.

The Atlantic and Pacific store, a business place in town,
and the post office is another place I've never been around.
There may be one or two more, that haven't it to sell.
But that, like lots of other things, is mighty hard to tell.

And last, but not least, a word from Dottie... written on an off day. And, after all, shouldn't a woman have the last word? Dare we have it otherwise?

TEASING?

I lost my sense of humor,
somewhere along the way.
Nothing ever seems funny,
throughout the whole long day.

Give me back or help me find
my sense of humor, once more.
Then you'll see me laugh again
'Cause I won't be feeling sore.

(maybe it was something you said?)

Nahhh! Not me, Plum.

Ted Leonard, seen here fleeing a mixed mob of critics, creditors and I.R.S. agents, is the author of two collections of Alaskan humor, *NOW! WE'RE HAVING FUN* and **ALASKAN WILD LIFE**, two Alaskan novels, **NEATH THE MIDNIGHT SUN** and **ALASKAN MAIL-ORDER BRIDE**, and this illustrated collection of Alaskan poetry **ARE WE HAVING FUN YET?** as well as numerous columns for several Alaskan newspapers.

Dear Ted,
Your two books, 'Now! We're Having Fun' and 'Alaskan Wild Life' are rich with the tongue in cheek type humor I enjoy so much. **Robin Heller, creator of MUKLUK**

This collection of wry anecdotes will strike a chord of fond appreciation in the heart of anyone familiar with — or anyone who would like to be familiar with — the special nature of living in Alaska. **Flip Todd, Alaska Book Distributors, Anchorage**

Reviewers' comments about Ted's first humor book NOW! WE'RE HAVING FUN:

"Alaska saga worth a read...a collection of droll, often self deprecating, tales... Leonard lives with wife "Sugarplum" in an off-road cabin, a rather upscale bush lifestyle that still provides its practitioners with myriad opportunities for things to go wrong. Leonard's gift is his ability to laugh about it." **Mike Dunham, Anchorage Daily News**

"Ted Leonard taught me all I know about Alaska, which is why I don't live there." **Dave Barry**

"The authorial voice is like that of a favorite uncle known for his storytelling, friendly and quite entertaining." **Carla Helfferich, FAIRBANKS ARTS**

"...Leonard is kind of a outdoors Dagwood Bumstead... I enjoyed several of Leonard's stories and his easy-going style" **Debbie Carter Fairbanks Daily News-Miner**